THE DEVIL

BUT
GOD

THE DEVIL HAD A PLAN...BUT GOD
Copyright © 2021 by Maranne Brookham

INTRODUCTION

The purpose of this book is to demonstrate how God intervened at just the right moments throughout my life – very strategic moments - crucial moments. At these times, God enveloped me in His love. At these times, He infused me with a new awareness of His presence and a deeper experience of Himself. At these times He brought me under a new level of His protection which would keep me during the next round of bad choices on my part. Each time He intervened, His plan was that I would leave the things of the world behind and go on with Him in a "sold out" relationship. I wish I could tell you that is what I did, but it took a long time for me to come to that place.

I want to demonstrate the faithfulness of God even when I was unfaithful; His goodness even when I was not good; His love even when I was unlovable; His grace even when I was wallowing in a sinful lifestyle.

If God is tugging on your heart now - respond now and do not delay. He will come into your life if you will simply invite Him in and He will turn your life around if you will give Him permission to do it. Please do not wait until your life is absolutely destroyed... turn to the Lord now and receive a new life with the old failures and ugliness of the past completely erased... be Born Again.

Romans 10:13 (NLT)
"For everyone who calls on the name of the LORD will be saved."

This is my story.

CHAPTER ONE

THE BEGINNING

I was born to a humble farming couple on the Canadian prairies. Life for them was scraping to make a living with little time for relaxation or pleasure. Neither of my parents had been raised in loving, nurturing families – life for both families was filled with responsibilities and hard work required to provide the essentials. Times were quite different in the early to mid 1900's.

We lived in a little house which was built in the common granary design with the addition of windows to provide light and some ventilation during the summer months. It was a two-roomed granary house – one was the kitchen with a table and chairs and a couple of "easy chairs" for company. There was a coal and wood stove that Mom used to produce very tasty meals, homemade bread, cakes and meat and fruit pies. There were cupboards made from butter boxes nailed together which were enhanced by colored cloth curtains. A huge crock kept the drinking water cool, when it was carried from the pump which seemed like miles from the house.

The second room in our granary house was the bedroom. There was a double bed for Mom and Dad and a metal crib in which I slept until I was probably three or four years old. The wall behind my crib was cupboards... oh, how I loved it when Mom said it was time to straighten the cupboards. I don't remember all that was kept in the cupboards, but I do remember that I felt it was like uncovering treasure as the contents were taken out and laid on the double bed. Blankets were re-folded and replaced in the cupboard; a few books were sorted and returned to the shelves; winter coats and boots were checked for buttons; and a few Christmas balls were admired and gently put back into their boxes. I'm sure there was more, but the pleasure was not in the quantity or grandness of the "things". The pleasure came in the warm memories which were stirred as we handled the contents of the cupboards. A card from a special day would serve to provide an opportunity to relive the joy. Pleasures were few and far between, so whether it came in the form of the first blooms of spring, a rainbow after the rain, a visit from a neighbour, a funny episode of a radio show, or a memento from days gone by – pleasure was welcome.

We had a big furry collie dog whose name was Sandy. He was my constant companion and friend. Together we explored the woods near our home, and he would lie quietly watching while I played in the pile of wood shavings in the yard. Sandy would accompany Mom and I as we walked the half-mile down the road to my Grandpa's home, where my two bachelor uncles lived too. This was something that Sandy and I enjoyed because it gave us the opportunity to explore different woods, old buildings, climb on machinery and have tea with my grandfather.

While we visited at Grandpa's house, Mom would do the laundry and ironing for our family and his. There was always work that took Mom and Dad away from me... housecleaning our home, Grandpa's house and Auntie Jeanetta's home which was in the yard at Grandpa's place. Auntie's home was another one of the popular two-roomed, granary houses with windows for light and ventilation in the summer months. Mom cooked the meals for Dad and my uncles who were busy with the field work; Grandpa did the gardening; so that left Auntie who was too old to do any of the work. She could not work BUT she loved to visit with me.

My early childhood would have been very lonely if not for my Auntie. She spent hours with me reading adult books to me (The Tale of Two Cities or another Dickens classic) and best of all, she read to me from her Bible and told me what to do with the devil when he tempted me to do bad things. She colored with me and held me on her knee covered in a blanket (even in the summer). She was not only an auntie, but a real friend, despite the age difference of some eighty years.

At some point when I was about five years old, the women in the district decided that it would be good to have Sunday School and take turns leading the lessons. I remember the newsprint lessons with pictures of Bible stories and singing old hymns of the church. I wanted to hear about God, because He represented love and I knew I wanted more love, more, more, more...

I think my family was what you would call religious, not Christian. I would hear them say "the Lord will take care of you" and Sundays we would listen on the radio to Alberta Premier Manning preach – but I do not think that faith really entered the picture. My folks were good people even though not loving and nurturing. They were worn out from their labor and did not have much energy left for affection and affirming a child.

I certainly knew what I could and could not do but not why I should not do it. There was lots of direction but very little instruction; lots of "go find something to play with" and very little "come and help me do this"; lots of "not now, I'm busy" and very little "come and sit with me". I know that my parents were doing the best they could and were doing what had been demonstrated to them by their parents. Now, I can say that I do not blame them for the loneliness and longing in my heart as a child. There was a familiarity in my life and routines, but there was not a feeling of security and safety...even as a young child I was fearful of being abandoned and being unprotected. In this insecurity, I found peace and hope in what I knew about God. Even as a very young child, I seemed to have an understanding or revelation of God that was much beyond my years. I believe that all people originate in the spiritual realm with God our Father, and that as young children we still have an awareness of that existence with Him.

When I was about four years old, I was walking with my Dad and he commented on how red the sky was. I remember my reply as though it was yesterday. I said, "It looks just like the day that Jesus died." My Dad cried, and I wondered why. I do not know why I said that, but I know that Jesus' death was real to me and important.

I knew God in those early years in a way that gave me a desire to know Him more and be with Him.

You see, the devil had a plan to bring destruction to my life through feelings of fear of danger and fear of being abandoned.... *but God* had a better plan.

God intervened with the love and instruction of my dear Auntie Jeanetta, who was thrilled to spend time with me and made me feel valued. He also intervened with Sunday School lessons and singing hymns which told me of my Father's love and about Jesus who loved me so much that He died on the cross to pay for all my sins.

God has a plan for each person, and it is a good plan. If you ask Him to show you His plan for your life, He will show you. Then ask Him to show you how to live His plan for you, and He will show you that too. Then He will even give you the strength and the wisdom you need to live in His will...just ask.

Matthew 7:7,8 (NLT)
"Keep on asking, and you will receive what you ask for. Keep on seeking, and you will find. Keep on knocking, and the door will be opened to you. For everyone who asks, receives. Everyone who seeks, finds. And to everyone who knocks, the door will be opened."

I encourage parents who may be reading this book - if you have young children who demonstrate a desire to know and live in relationship with God, support them in it and guide them in scripture and prayer. Young children can know God, and in fact long to reconnect with their Heavenly Father from whom they came. Remember Samuel who began to hear from the Lord at a very early age and prophesied to the High Priest, Eli. 1Samuel 2:18 (NLT) "But Samuel, though he was only a boy, served the Lord."

CHAPTER TWO

STILL LOST IN THE BUSYNESS

You will remember that I said I had the comfort of the familiar while I was a young child on the farm, although there was not a strong sense of security and being loved. The comfort of the familiar was about to end abruptly, and a new level of loneliness and fear would become my experience.

This life-changing upheaval was brought about by a visit to the bank to withdraw money to purchase a few groceries. The teller revealed the grim facts. There was a balance of twenty-five cents in my parents account...certainly not enough to buy groceries - not enough for anything. As we sat in the cab of our old International truck, my parents wondering between them what they would do, there was another of those *but God* moments. Down the street came an auntie - my Dad's sister - who gave my parents twenty silver dollars. This was plenty to buy the groceries needed for the moment; however, my parents decided that something must be done to change the situation in a lasting sort of way...it was decided that we would move into town so that my Mom could find work and it would be within driving distance for Dad to drive back and forth to continue farming.

Where would we live? Where would I go to school? Will I be safe there? Who will be with me when my parents are at work? All these questions and no answers; all these fears and no comfort.... what about my dog Sandy? Will he know that I still love him, will he understand that people in the city do not want a big old farm dog living in their house. What will I do when I am lonely?

The first place we moved was another of those granary houses that seemed to be wherever we were. The only difference was that it was in the city and not on the farm that I was familiar with and which I loved. We stayed there a short time, but because of the long walk for my Mom to and from her work, we found another place closer for her.

We lived in the upstairs apartment of a lovely and respectable house which was owned by a lovely and respectable elderly couple. They were kind and peaceful people. They made us feel very welcome and extended themselves in many ways to us.

The apartment had a kitchen, living room, and a bedroom. We shared the bathroom which was on the main floor. I slept on the couch in the living room, but it felt quite luxurious because it was furnished with nice furniture - not like what we had at the farm. Quite honestly, it felt like a mansion, and the best part was that our landlords offered their piano if I would like to take piano lessons. I could practice, using their piano for as long as we lived in their apartment. It was too good to be true. I loved music and practicing was joy.

It was on one of those long evenings when I was the only one home, that I had an incredible experience. I was practicing my piano homework and the only light that was on in the house was the piano light. The rest of the house was in darkness and something caught my eye. I looked over into the dining room and saw a huge angel which gave light to the dining room. He was very tall, and I could not see his head as it reached to the ceiling. He was clothed in shining white robes and it was not a fearful experience at all. I had never seen an angel before but knew immediately that this was an angel. I had complete peace and knew instinctively that He would not harm me... another of those *but God* moments to equip me for the next leg of my journey. It could have brought me great peace and security if I had reminded myself of the encounter more often than I did.

I look back on this home and our landlords with gratefulness for their warmth and example. They were quiet people who enjoyed a peaceful life together. They did not argue or use bad language – they just lived together in harmony. It is a part of my childhood that I remember with good feelings, and even though I was alone much of the time, I was not lonely or anxious. It was also here that we purchased our first TV set... what glorious fun! When Mom and Dad and I were home, sometimes we would watch the Ed Sullivan Show. It felt like a dream come true, but dreams end, and you wake up to a new day.

The new day came, and it was time to move again because I needed to have a bedroom of my own. We moved to a nice basement suite which was quite close to work for my Mom. This was important since she worked shifts and walked home at midnight often.

This new neighborhood was quiet and respectable and there was a family who lived across the street from us who had kids about my age. This was another of those *but God* moments...

One day when we (kids) were getting acquainted, they asked if I would like to go to church with them. Their parents had agreed, and I was to ask my parents. My parents agreed as well, and I started going to church with my new friends. I enjoyed the Sunday school lessons and the singing of the hymns, but one Sunday evening there was a guest speaker. The kids could come, and they invited me to join them.

I do not remember what the speaker said, but I remember the feeling inside while I was listening. It was like there was something I knew I needed to do, but I didn't know what that something was. Finally, the speaker gave an "Altar Call" for anyone who wanted to invite Jesus into their heart...at that moment I knew what it was that I needed to do. I went to the altar, not knowing what to expect. The Pastor's wife came up and took me aside into a Sunday school room and asked what I knew about God and the Lord Jesus. She asked if I had ever prayed, and I told her that I said the Lord's prayer at night, and she led me in what I know now to be the Sinner's Prayer...I was only nine or ten, but I knew I needed Jesus in my heart. It was such a relief that came over me when I prayed with the pastor's wife. It was real, and I knew it was real.

The next day was Monday and I told my friends at school about what happened to me the night before. I told them that they needed Jesus to come into their heart also. My heart was so full of excitement and joy! You see, God knew I needed to be saved for the next leg of my journey. I needed to be covered by His protection for what was coming.

The devil had a plan to destroy my life, but God had another plan...

The devil wanted to keep me isolated and lonely so that he would have clear access to my mind. God brought friends into my life who would be instrumental in bringing me to a relationship with Jesus.

2 Corinthians 6:2 (NLT)
"For God says,
"At just the right time, I heard you.
On the day of salvation, I helped you. "Indeed, the
"right time" is now. Today is the day of salvation."

If you are experiencing that stirring in your heart as you read my story, that is God saying that today is the day of salvation. If you feel that there is something you need to do – THERE IS!

You need to invite Jesus to come into your heart and forgive your sins. Tell Him that you are tired of the old ways of living and are ready for the new beginning He can give you. Do not delay...do it now and be born again.

CHAPTER THREE

THE TRAP

The days and months after inviting Jesus into my heart were important in my journey because I found myself drawing into a relationship with Jesus. I continued to attend church with my friends across the street. We spent time together after school each day, and there was a feeling of security and peace when we were together. They were a family that left a lasting mark upon me, and to this day I remember with gratefulness their passing through my life...they were another *but God* situation for me.

Well, a pattern developed in my family's life since moving to the city. We would settle in and we would discover that we had need of more room or more privacy or a quieter setting so that Mom could sleep during the day when she was working afternoon or night shifts. Again, we needed a change of accommodations...but this time it meant not only a change of residence. This time I had friends and it meant moving away from them and moving away from them meant I would no longer be able to attend church.

As I mentioned earlier, my folks were religious rather than Christians. Christians have a relationship with the Lord – religious people follow rules. Since moving to the city, it seemed that the weekly radio sermons and discussions that followed became a thing of the past. It seemed that the influence of the world was pushing its way into the lives of my parents. I heard less that the Lord was watching over us and more about the people and situations that Mom encountered working in the institution for mentally handicapped people. I missed my "church friends" and I discovered that I was lonely. Mom and Dad were not able to provide the spiritual support and encouragement which I received from my friends.

After moving, my loneliness caused me to draw upon my new life in Jesus, and it was then that the Lord placed His call upon me. I knew that I was called to preach, and that is what I did. I set up my "pulpit" on my dresser and placed my Bible and hymnal side by side...I would preach into the mirror of my dresser and lead worship from the hymnal. The "services" I enacted were filling a spiritual need as well as filling the long and lonely hours I spent each day. I believe that the time I spent "preaching" was building a strength in me for the dangerous times ahead, and the hymns of worship developed assurance of His love and that He would never leave me.

When I was about 10 or eleven, I was given household duties and cooking responsibilities. Although these duties took some time, there was still ample time to experience the loneliness which grew stronger and more demanding of my attention. It filled our house and waited for me to get home from school to envelope me in its cold, dark presence. Even when I was at school, I would dread going home.

Every person needs the acceptance and involvement of other human beings. This need was becoming greater and greater, and I was desperate for love and acceptance. I was becoming a young lady and had no instruction in modesty or any other social skills. Having been isolated as a child on the farm and being an only child, raised around adults and mostly men, I was without a foundation to build upon. I was floundering and seeking anything to which I could attach myself...in such matters, the devil is very accommodating. He provided a family to lay the trap without their knowledge.

I was now twelve years old with all the issues of a twelve-year-old and none of the nurture and instruction of a well-equipped parent. This is the recipe for disaster and heartache.

Disaster came in the form of a harmless looking request by a family with four children. The parents approached me about babysitting for them. I knew nothing about children and my first thought was, "well, I guess I can take a bath when I get home." At that time, I thought children were dirty little beasts.

It turned out that the disaster was not looking after the children, but in the ensuing relationship I developed with the parents...remember I was an adult for all intents and purposes, except that I did not have the emotional maturity of an adult. I was a broken vessel.

This was a time when substances and chemicals were not locked up and accounted for. The husband in this family worked in hospital maintenance and had access to cans of rubbing alcohol. On the weekends, he would come home with a gallon of rubbing alcohol and Tom Collins Mix. It was then I was introduced to the numbing effects of alcohol...I discovered an escape from the pain of loneliness which was becoming depression. Whenever I had the chance to "drown my sorrows" I went all in. There was no measure of using alcohol for social purposes – I drank to get drunk and forget everything.

Now, all of this sounds remarkably heavy and dark, and it was but, I want to point out the *but God* factor that was taking place through this time. Rubbing alcohol can be fatal when consumed in large amounts; it can produce brain damage and even blindness. I suffered none of these issues.

When I went forward to receive Jesus into my heart three years earlier, His protection also became mine. Promises found in the Word of God now were mine.

Isaiah 54:17(KNJV)
"No weapon formed against you shall prosper,
And every tongue which rises against you in judgment
you shall condemn.
This is the heritage of the servants of the LORD,
And their righteousness is from Me,"
Says the LORD."

You may say, "what weapon, what are you talking about"?

Well, the devil is the enemy of God and of those who belong to Him. He is full of schemes and weapons to defeat God's children. The weapon he used on me was the alcohol...he wanted to kill me or at least dis-able me to prevent the plans of God from being accomplished in my life. Satan knows the best way to hurt God is to hurt His children!

Psalm 34:7(NLT)
"The angel of the LORD encamps all around those who
fear Him, And delivers them."

I was making extremely poor decisions at this stage of my life; however, they were decisions I made being naïve and without instruction. God's provision of protection was mine because when I was "born again", I became His child. He loved and protected me, even though I did not always remember that. It was God's protection that prevailed, and I escaped what could have been...Praise God!

> John 10:10 (NLT) (Jesus speaking)
> *"The thief's purpose is to steal and kill and destroy. My purpose is to give them a rich and satisfying life." This is explaining the vast and opposite purpose of the devil and Jesus.*

When Satan introduced me to alcohol, his intent was to steal my freedom; kill me physically; or destroy my life and lead me into a depraved lifestyle that would not reflect the image of God.... *but God* had another and much better plan.

The life God had for me was to serve him by preaching/teaching the Gospel and evangelism. I began to lose my focus on the Lord and the relationship that I had begun to build with Him. Over time, I became more ensnared in the world and the search for ways to rid myself of the loneliness and depression that were taking over more of my waking hours. From this place of desperation, I felt unable to continue the routine of life - school, house duties, homework, trying to relate to people. I withdrew by skipping weeks of school; retreating into an internal world of fantasy where I would find myself loved; and indulging in my new numbing substance ~ food. I added this new substance to the previous arsenal of alcohol in various forms.

Finally, after months of agony, my parents became aware that all the discipline in the world and insisting I attend school could not force me to "be happy". I was sent to the family doctor who in turn sent me to a psychiatrist.

This was during the years when psychiatric drugs were being used freely without a great deal of monitoring. I was prescribed a very strong medication which was used for years to control epileptic seizures...phenobarbital...which is also extremely addictive and leaves you unable to think clearly and engage in life.

I cannot say whether it was months or a year or more that I spent in that place of just existing...I was not connected to my surroundings or to the people around me. I was not conscious of the passage of time or emotions...it was a place and that is all...a place of nothingness. Often now, as I go about my daily duties, I see people who are living in that same place. They are those souls who shuffle from place to place completing a routine of chores or duties without any of the pleasant feelings that others experience from similar activities...those who exist without really living because of medication intended to increase their quality of life!

The next *but God* moment came about one afternoon when I had shuffled off to the pharmacy to fill my prescription. I was shuffling home quite unaware of anything going on around me, when I heard a male voice behind me say, "Throw those away now!" I recognized the "heavenly" quality to this voice. It was not frightening, and I simply obeyed. Just as when the angel had allowed me to see him when I was playing the piano as a young child, this angelic voice allowed me to hear him.

I still remember the storm drain and the very corner in my hometown, where I obeyed the voice and threw those pills away.

God further intervened by preventing any withdrawal from this very addictive and thought hindering medication ~ I just obeyed, and I was released. Although I continued to experience bouts of depression, they were never as severe as this experience. Over the years, I have learned how to take my authority in Christ over depression, and to praise God for His goodness to me...then depression must leave. (2Timothy 2:26 (NLT) "Then they will come to their senses and escape from the devil's trap. For they have been held captive by him to do whatever he wants.")

I was now about fourteen years old and this was the age for confirmation in the life of young people being raised in the Anglican faith. I was not being raised in any faith per se; but Mom and Dad still saw themselves as Anglican. They approached the minister at a local Anglican church to enroll me into the Catechism classes to prepare for Confirmation. The purpose of the Confirmation of youth is for the Holy Spirit to fill them for their life ahead.

The minister and his wife were very Christian people who had experienced the infilling of the Holy Spirit with the sign of speaking in tongues, which is unusual in the Anglican church. Again, God was intervening at a crucial time in my life.

During the Catechism classes, the minister (during individual sessions) talked to me about what I could experience during Confirmation. He talked to me about saying words I do not know, and perhaps feeling "something" when the Bishop laid hands on us. I did not fully understand what he was explaining to me; however, at the service I experienced a presence of God I had not known before. I felt weak and began to shake and sob when Bishop laid hands on me. I remember, even now, the impact of that event...although I did not speak in tongues, I know that the Holy Spirit came upon me and I was again strengthened for what was coming.

CHAPTER FOUR

THE WILDERNESS YEARS

During the next years, I am ashamed to say that I seldom called on the Lord, and then only when I needed to be rescued from some desperate situation, but for the most part I ignored Him. God is always faithful even when we are not - He is faithful. He never gives up on us and waits patiently for us to remember Him. As a born-again person, we are His child and He will never abandon us. We belong to Him.

> Isaiah 43:1(NLT)
> ".... listen to the Lord who created you....."Do not be afraid, for I have ransomed you. I have called you by name; you are mine."

School continued to be a difficult setting for me. I had one friend with whom I felt comfortable and enjoyed quite a close relationship; however, outside of this friendship, school was hostile territory.

At the end of grade ten, I informed my Mom that I would not be going back to high school. She then informed me that I would be completing my education somewhere. She made phone calls and an appointment was set for me to apply to a college about an hour away.

The dean of the college had explained to Mom that only if I were able to pass the entrance exam, would I be allowed to attend college there. I wrote the exam and passed ...I would be attending college in the fall.

The year flew by and I enjoyed being away from home. There were all kinds of frivolous and hilarious experiences, but not many hours spent in studying and applying myself to the business of learning.

During that year, I met a young man who asked me to marry him. I knew I did not love him and that he was not right for me; however, marriage would be a way to escape my home life. I accepted.

The alcohol I had been introduced to five years earlier was still providing the relief from pain and sense of impending doom. Although I was not a daily drunk, I could not drink without getting "falling-down drunk". I drank with one purpose in mind – lose myself and find that place of nothingness that the medication had taken me to in the past. The man who asked me to marry him had the same kind of relationship with alcohol...we were a recipe for destruction.

After we were married, booze became a frequent visitor in our home. The people we associated with were participants in the same kind of lifestyle. Drinking was now a part of all our activities and with the drinking came outbursts of temper and eventually, physical violence began to segregate us from those we once did life with.

Our first daughter, Lea, was born on a very cold winter day and I wondered how I would be able to manage with a child to raise...what did that mean anyway? I had very little experience with children and felt uneasy at the prospect.

This beautiful little person seemed from the first, to be at odds with me...she was very colicky. Nothing seemed to quiet her screams, except going for a ride in the car; however, car rides cannot go on forever. Looking back now, she was probably sensing my nervousness and strong emotion.

I did not understand the role a parent should play in the life of a child. I had only what had been modeled for me by my parents. The distance they demonstrated to me was only what they had known from their parents. I do not believe they intended to neglect or abuse me, however, the result was the same.

This was the beginning of another generation of this parent-child relationship which was compounded by the hostility I perceived my infant daughter was demonstrating towards me. Due to this faulty and unrealistic perception I began to respond to my daughter as though it were true. I was harsh in relating to her and did not nurture her in the ways that I craved as a little person...I was repeating the cycle. I hated the coldness with which I treated my daughter and I tried to change my parenting methods; however, I was just as powerless over this part of my life as I was over the bouts of drunkenness. What was I to do? I felt trapped in this mess, and my mind was in constant turmoil.

My husband became a slave to alcohol and with the slavery came a great rage that he expressed increasingly more often – sometimes there was brawling in bars or with family members and sometimes it was directed at me.

I, too, had experienced rage since my teen years. It was the same rage that my Dad had demonstrated often over the course of my life at home and since. Life is cyclical and requires a choice to stop destructive cycles and to seek help from the only One able to deliver us – God.

I continued to use alcohol and prescription drugs to numb the pain and disgust I felt as I lived my life trapped and I could not break free. I wanted to be a good parent...I wanted to be free of alcohol and medication...I wanted to be respectable...I wanted peace...I wanted a good marriage...I wanted what seemed to be out of my reach.

I became pregnant again but did not understand the danger of drinking during pregnancy, since there was no research in this area that was readily available. I'm not sure that I would have refrained from drinking even if I did know. I really was a person that even I could not respect! People who saw my drinking and brawling and coarse behavior would have thought me "human trash". They saw what was evident on the outside. On the inside, I was broken and hurting...longing to be different.

My second daughter, Lynne, was born, and I felt an immediate bond with her. She seemed different somehow. She seemed willing to allow me to love her, not colicky like my first daughter. It was just a few months later, that we discovered that she was not developing as quickly as other babies. The term Fetal Alcohol Effect was not yet known, at least to me. This was the beginning of a life of struggle for her. She struggled to learn things which other children learned easily; however, she was tenacious. She just plugged away at life with a mischievous humour.

Our family doctor advised us to have Lynne assessed by a team of psychologists, speech therapists, and occupational therapists. This resulted in a several month's stay at a Rehabilitation Hospital which was a couple of hours from our home. We were not permitted to visit for the first three or four weeks of her stay. She was only four years old and my heart broke for our little daughter away from all that was familiar.

When she came home at the end of her rehabilitation (behavior modification), she was a little robot, doing things by rote and not by inspiration of her own initiation. She had been placed on medication to make her more "train-able" and she was emotionally flat...she did not seem to enjoy or reject anything. This little person was a stranger to me, so I set about weaning her off the medication and decided I would teach her what I could. Over time, she began to take on a personality and she expressed joy, frustration, love, and anger...she was becoming an expressive person. She had developed quite an extensive vocabulary, but she lacked internal controls. This resulted in non-stop talking and extremely poor volume control. I felt as though I was living in a pressure cooker...out of control.

Lea, our eldest daughter, was blossoming. She was a very bright child and enjoyed life with all its possibilities. She was healthy and beautiful and filled our home with life...sometimes way too much life for me.

I would lose control during these stressful times; and rather than quiet explanations, I would yell and discipline the girls harshly – I was perpetuating a pattern from my childhood without realizing it.

As a backdrop to the early years of our daughters, we were living in our own personal hell. My husband was in a perpetual state of drunkenness and anger. He became a tyrant who would not permit laughter or noisy play in the house. The girls and I were prisoners when he was home. It was a very oppressive existence.

The next few years continued in this very destructive pattern of violence and horrible threats. We were living in a war zone...what an awful environment for children in those early, tender years!

At first, my husband's violence was levelled against others outside our marriage; however, eventually it made its way into our marriage. I was now an abused wife... abused in ways I did not even know existed...abused in every way a woman can be abused.

The rage was increasing, and I found myself becoming angry more often now, and the outbursts were more violent. I would break things in the house in a fit of drunken rage and cut my feet in the morning as I stepped into the mess I made the night before. Scenes like this would remind me of the wreck I was making of my life and the lives of our daughters. The abuse continued and became more intense and the craziness of the situation left me doubting my own sanity.

We were increasingly more isolated from friends we once had and family members who could no longer bear to see what we had become; that is, except for one couple. They were a sister-in-law and her husband. Many hours and weekends had been spent with them, doing the same things that had become a trap to us.

Often, my sister-in-law and I would make a Ouija board and spend the afternoon communicating with "the dark side". We believed what we were doing was simply a form of entertainment, and we continued. However, one afternoon was different...we received an answer from the other side and Suzanna had a physical manifestation in her body. She screamed and asked me to take the Ouija board out and break it. She said that something had happened to her and I could see that she believed that. After that, she became ill and was told that they could not find the cause of her symptoms. The doctors told her husband that if they could not turn her situation around, she would die...*but God!*!

Through a series of God-ordained events, she was taken to a church service where she was ministered to and delivered from the plans of the devil to kill her.

She and her husband were born-again and filled with the Holy Spirit. They were changed in a marvelous and very visible way. Their language changed; they no longer needed or used alcohol or any other substance we had used previously; and they treated their children differently. This change made my husband incredibly angry, and he was the one who distanced us from them.

The change in them was a magnet to me, however. It brought back memories of my earlier childhood and my desire to know God and feel close to Him once more.

Jeremiah 3:22 (NLT)
"My wayward children," says the Lord, "come back to me, and I will heal your wayward hearts."

My heart was beginning to be open once more to the voice of the Lord...I was again hungering for Him. I could sense that He was calling me to return from my wandering. This time, God was using a *but God* moment in someone else's life to influence me.

Perhaps you once invited the Lord into your life and had begun to walk with Him; however, poor decisions distanced you from His wonderful presence. It is not too late – return to Him NOW!! He will not reject you.

Luke 15:11 – 32 (NLT)
"To illustrate the point further, Jesus told them this story: "A man had two sons. The younger son told his father, 'I want my share of your estate now before you die.' So his father agreed to divide his wealth between his sons. A few

days later this younger son packed all his belongings and moved to a distant land, and there he wasted all his money in wild living. About the time his money ran out, a great famine swept over the land, and he began to starve. He persuaded a local farmer to hire him, and the man sent him into his fields to feed the pigs. The young man became so hungry that even the pods he was feeding the pigs looked good to him. But no one gave him anything. When he finally came to his senses, he said to himself, 'At home even the hired servants have food enough to spare, and here I am dying of hunger! I will go home to my father and say, "Father, I have sinned against both heaven and you, and I am no longer worthy of being called your son. Please take me on as a hired servant."' "So, he returned home to his father. And while he was still a long way off, his father saw him coming. Filled with love and compassion, he ran to his son, embraced him, and kissed him. His son said to him, 'Father, I have sinned against both heaven and you, and I am no longer worthy of being called your son. But his father said to the servants, 'Quick! Bring the finest robe in the house and put it on him. Get a ring for his finger and sandals for his feet."

If you are in the same circumstances as the son Jesus told about, now is the time to go back to your Father. He will give you the same welcome that the father in this account gave his son. Ask God to forgive you and put Him back on the throne of your life.

His Love is everlasting, and He forgives every sincere person...you will be welcomed and there will be great rejoicing in Heaven because you have come home...do not wait – *do it Now.*

CHAPTER FIVE

THE RESCUE

As I previously mentioned, my husband was not about to be "preached at" by his sister and her husband. Just the idea that they had become Christians, in his mind made them "religious fanatics" who were stalking helpless prey. He refused to visit with them or even speak on the phone to them. I, on the other hand, welcomed running into them on the street, and occasionally, I would phone Suzanna. She would tell me about the ways that God was changing them and the wonderful truth they were learning in the church they were attending.

Over the years, we had discussed our beliefs, and I told her about my experience being born-again as a young child. One day, we chatted about the usual topics of our conversations and I mentioned my struggles to be free from the lifestyle I was trapped in. She became really serious and said "You need to get right with God. You know the way, and you know what to do." She said that she and her husband were heading for hell before they got saved, and that did it...I said I needed to go. I hung up the phone and knelt on the kitchen floor. I cried out to God...really cried out to God. I prayed a prayer that went something like ~ "God, I believe You're real and that You are able to help me. I have tried to get clean for years and tried to become a good parent...I do not know how. I want to live for You. Please set me free. I believe in You. Amen" (I really did not know much about prayer at that point; but what I said, I meant with my whole heart. That is all that is required when you pray...you do not need to use fancy language or read it out of a book. Just talk to God like you would talk to someone you respect; someone you want to spend time with.)

Well, that was what I said and how it happened; but what unfolded after that prayer is totally amazing! When I stood up, I knew I had been set free. I had no fear that I would fall back into the ways of drinking and substance abuse and parenting the old way. I was free, and I knew it! Drinking and use of substances were a thing of the past from that moment and an utterly new life was given to me. I discovered real love for my children and began to have fun with them and treat them with patience and kindness. God is so great and so faithful ~ Praise His Name!

It was like living a life that I had previously only dreamed about. Joy filled my life, and I began to read my Bible. I read it, not because I felt I had to, but because I wanted to...I fell in love with the Word of God!

My life had been radically changed by the Love and Power of God. I welcomed the changes that God was making almost daily; however, my husband became consumed with anger against this God who had taken away the familiarity of his marriage. He became bitter and even more controlling than before. The abuse went to a whole new level, and I began to feel I was losing my sanity. The only thing that was real to me was Jesus and my love for the precious Word of God and my new-found relationship with my daughters.

The Lord taught me to be a mama who took joy in her children and I learned to nurture them, and I taught them about Jesus. I would read Bible stories to them at bedtime and then we would pray together. The girls wanted to know about Jesus, and I am sure they saw a vast difference in me and the way I related to them. In a noticeably short time, both girls said they wanted to ask Jesus into their heart. I had the privilege of leading both daughters into the kingdom of God. Lea was about seven years old, and Lynne was about five.

The situation in my marriage was beyond words...I was not permitted to read the Bible or leave it where my husband could see it. I had to be secretive about my relationship with Jesus, but it did not destroy my desire to live for the Lord. When Lynne began school, I found I had time to read the Word and pray...these were glorious times in His presence. I learned to hear the voice of my Shepherd, and I was confident in the love that God had for me. It kept me!

Lynne began pre-school in the early intervention program, to address learning difficulties she had. I went into the classroom as a parent volunteer. This was very fulfilling for me and I decided to attend college in January in the Early Childhood Program.

There were so many wonderful things taking place in my life in a short time. The Lord had set me free from the trap the enemy had set for me many years before, and life had taken on new meaning. Now, my daughters had a relationship with Jesus also...what joy! God is so loving and giving; and He delights in blessing us.

One of His blessings came during the times I spent volunteering in the classroom...the teacher pointed out that I related well to the children and invited me to be part-time classroom aide. I was overjoyed...all my life I had heard that I was a loser and had no potential. Someone was seeing in me something I was totally unaware of – I had something to offer!

Now I was more determined than ever to attend college in the winter session. My husband fought to maintain control over his household – not only was his wife a "religious fanatic" but she was going to become more educated. At the time, I did not know that abusive people are threatened when the person they are abusing begins to make decisions and develop as a person.

My husband saw my relationship with Jesus as a threat to his control over me, and he saw my going to college as a further threat. Tension in our home was at a pinnacle...rules became more restrictive and abuse against me escalated.

As I read the Bible and spent time in prayer, I became aware that I wanted more in my relationship with Jesus. I still occasionally dared to phone my sister-in-law and told her how I was feeling. She told me about being filled with the Holy Spirit with the evidence of speaking with other tongues. She described to me what my spirit was craving...a further closeness with God...a deeper walk with Him.

I continued to work in the kindergarten and spent many hours studying the scriptures about being baptized in the Holy Spirit...oh, how I longed for this. As January drew closer, I knew that going to college coupled with the tension at home would be too much for me, unless... unless I had the inner strength which accompanied the baptism of the Spirit of God.

I prayed asking God to lead me to the book which would lead me into the teaching I was seeking. After I prayed, I went immediately to our local Bible bookstore.... another *but God* moment was approaching!

I walked down the stairs into the bookstore, and as I went, I prayed "God, please lead me to the right book; You know exactly what I need".

I was walking through one section to go to the information desk when I heard a book fall to the floor. I walked over to put it back. I looked at the book in my hand and what I saw blew me away...the title of the book was "The Holy Spirit and You" by Dennis and Rita Bennett. There must have been an angel on assignment dropping that book to the floor when I would hear it fall. So many times, people say, "it was such a coincidence!" when it was really an orchestrated plan of God involving angels or other people.

I do not believe in coincidences; I believe in God events. This incident fully convinced me that God heard my prayer, that He loved me enough to answer me in a wonderful way, and that He wanted me to receive all that He had for me – even the infilling of the Holy Spirit.

I began reading the book on my first free afternoon while the girls were at school. It was set out in just the way I needed to be taught...it led the reader through a process, beginning with salvation. Each chapter took me to a deeper understanding with a prayer at the end of each section.

There was a chapter which talked about occult practices – remember the Ouija board? I read the chapter and prayed the prayer renouncing my involvement in this practice. On and on I read, reading each section, and praying the prayer at the end. Finally, I got to the chapter on being filled with the Holy Spirit! I was so excited – at last I would receive the gift I had been seeking.

I read the chapter, and I was about to pray the prayer written there. I was home alone, but I felt I should lock myself in the bathroom just in case I got loud. I had no idea what this would be like because I had not been allowed to attend church. I had no idea what it would sound like or how it would happen. What excitement!

I took the book into the bathroom and locked the door. I sat on the edge of the tub and read the prayer from the pages. I asked God to give me tongues in a song because of my love of music...and what happened was beyond amazing! I opened my mouth in faith and started to make sounds - out came the most beautiful song in a language I did not know. The tune was "heavenly", and the language flowed...I received the gift I was seeking - Praise God!

I spoke often and for long periods in the wonderful language I had been given. I began to hear God's voice in my heart telling me that He loved me and that He was pleased with me. The Word of God became alive to me and the Lord spoke to me as I studied the Word.

I was learning about the Holy Spirit who had taken up residence inside me, giving me strength for each day and filling me with the Love of God – love for people; love for animals; love for creation; love filled me and flowed out from me towards others. (Romans 5:5, NLT) "And this hope will not lead to disappointment. For we know how dearly God loves us, because he has given us the Holy Spirit to fill our hearts with his love.

Life went to a whole new level. I had an inner strength I did not have before being baptized in the Holy Spirit. When there was great turmoil in our home, I had a joy that did not depend on my circumstances. When I spoke, I recognized a new wisdom and understanding which I discovered are gifts of the Holy Spirit. I found that I saw beyond someone's behavior to the spiritual reason for the behavior. (Romans 11:33a, NLT) "Oh, how great are God's riches and wisdom and knowledge! How impossible it is for us to understand his decisions and his ways!"

I began to study the scriptures which taught on the gifts of the Holy Spirit, and I found books about people being used in the gifts. This new facet of my life was so rich and fulfilling and I revelled in the depth of my relationship with the Lord.

1 Corinthians 12:4-12 (NLT) excerpts

"There are different kinds of spiritual gifts, but the same Spirit is the source of them all. There are different kinds of service, but we serve the same Lord. 6 God works in different ways, but it is the same God who does the work in all of us. A spiritual gift is given to each of us so we can help each other. To one person the Spirit gives the ability to give wise advice[a]; to another the same Spirit gives a message of special knowledge. The same Spirit gives great faith to another, and to someone else the one Spirit gives the gift of healing. He gives one person the power to perform miracles, and another the ability to prophesy. He gives someone else the ability to discern whether a message is from the Spirit of God or from another spirit. Still another person is given the ability to speak in unknown languages, while another is given the ability to interpret what is being said. It is the one and only Spirit who distributes all these gifts. He alone decides which gift each person should have. The human body has many parts, but the many parts make up one whole body. So it is with the body of Christ."

I wanted God to use me to bring the message of forgiveness and restoration to others who were still trapped in the lifestyle I had come from...I remembered the "call to preach" I received when I was around ten or twelve years old. This burned stronger in my heart than ever, but I had no idea how it would happen. It seemed impossible as I looked at my life – how in the world could it possibly happen?

I continued to attend college part-time and part-time I worked in the classroom. I was fulfilled in both places...I was getting good grades and I enjoyed using my newly acquired knowledge with the children at school.

The girls were growing in their faith in Jesus as we read the Word, enjoyed Bible stories, and prayed together each day. I saw the difference the Lord makes in people of all ages.

During this time, as I was growing in the Word and in my relationship with the Lord, I longed to be part of a church – *but God* was teaching me even in our isolation. Often, as I read the "church pages" in our local newspaper, titles for sermons would reflect what God had taught me during the week. I was blown away that God would teach me at home what congregations throughout the city would be learning on Sunday morning. God is so faithful!

I asked my husband often (probably too often) to take us to church and finally after months of pleading, he consented to go to the traditional church that he had been raised in. It was not a place you could hear about salvation, so my husband was comfortable there for a short time, and the girls were able to attend Sunday school with other children. As for myself, I experienced God's presence in the words of the liturgy and creeds...I believe that if you are looking for God, you will find Him, no matter what denomination is on the door!

After my husband lost interest in church, we did not attend anywhere for a time; however, I asked if I could take the girls to church somewhere since they were missing it. He finally consented, and I took them to a Spirit-filled church where we could see the Holy Spirit move through the pastor and the people. It was amazing! My zeal for God and connection with His people sky rocketed. I was so grateful that God had made this possible. Even in the battlefield in our home and marriage, God was able to bring answers to my prayers.

I confided in my pastor and his wife about the types of abuse I was experiencing at home; however, at that time the church (the whole body of Christ) had not come to the revelation it has today. I was told that I must stay since I was the Christian party in the marriage.

I determined that I would stay and "come boldly to the throne of grace and obtain mercy in times of need."

CHAPTER SIX

No Rules of Engagement (The Devil Fights Dirty)

I want to remind the reader of the title of my story, "the devil had a plan....*but God*." This was another of those times just unfolding in the life of our eldest daughter. As you will recall, Lea was a very bright girl and full of life. I noticed some very odd behaviours and physical movements. I took her to our family doc due to the severe mood swings she was experiencing. She had also developed a slightly awkward gait. The doctor said that she was probably just experiencing symptoms that accompany puberty. We accepted that for a time; however, the symptoms became more pronounced...back to the doc. By now, she had developed a slur in her speech and sometimes she would drool.

We were confused by the change we saw taking place in our daughter, and of course, genuinely concerned. We had no idea the serious nature of this condition that was emerging.

One day, after being out for a walk, Lea said she was feeling nauseous, and she leaned over the kitchen sink. What happened next was more than I could comprehend... our daughter vomited huge chunks of congealed blood that looked like her liver. Lynne, our youngest daughter began praying in tongues and we called 911. The ambulance was there almost immediately, and we followed the ambulance to the hospital. This was New Years Eve and we were told that it would be a long wait until a doctor would arrive...*enter God*!

Remember that I do not believe in coincidences... there was a Paediatric Specialist who had not left for the evening, and he said he would assess the patient – our daughter. This specialist just happened to be a Christian, and he took all the time he needed to make his diagnosis and recommendations.

After a very lengthy examination and hours of questions, the doctor said that he believed Lea had Wilson's Disease; however, he could not be positive since he had never seen it before. It turned out that this disease is so rare that it is considered an orphan disease and extraordinarily little research had been done on it.

Lea was only the thirteenth person to be diagnosed with Wilson's Disease ever in (I believe he said) western Canada. The doctor said that she would need to be transferred to the University Hospital where she would be seen by specialists who would be able to accurately identify the disease.

At the University Hospital, the diagnosis was confirmed, and it was decided that Lea would be started on the only treatment that they were aware of at the time. The doctor told us that if we were people who prayed, now would be the time, since the treatment was a medication from WWI. It was used to treat soldiers who had inhaled Mustard Gas. It was a very severe drug and exacerbated the symptoms before and if it improved them. At this juncture, there was a possibility that Lea would not survive the treatment...I *prayed*...Lynne *prayed*!

The treatment was begun, and within a day or two Lea had gone from being able to walk and talk and eat to being unable to do any of these things. She laid in one position in the hospital bed, not being able to swallow, with her arms and legs drawn up to her body...this was *treatment*?

We were told that we should go home and get some rest and visit as we were able. We drove the two hours home in disbelief. My husband did not have the benefit of a relationship with the Lord, so his only coping skill was getting drunk...a drunk that lasted for several years.

While we were at home, I worked and attended church...it was business as usual, that is, with a huge hole in my heart which was the uncertainty of our daughter's future. One of my friends from church called the same week Lea's treatment was started. She said that she found an article in the "Saturday Evening Post' that week about a woman in the United States with the same disease Lea had! Coincidence you say – I think not!

I read the first episode and got the next week's edition when it came out. The woman had given her contact information in the final episode. I was all over that. I called her, and when we talked, it was like talking to my daughter. Her speech was so like Lea's. This lady (Joan) had been admitted to a mental institution because of the same symptoms we had seen in Lea; and an astute resident who came to do rounds, took the time to dig a little deeper and discovered the tell-tale rings in Joan's eyes – Keiser-Fleischer rings.

The diagnosis of Wilson's Disease was made, and she was put on a cutting-edge treatment which was making great improvement in her life.

Joan was pleased that her story was reaching people who needed the information and she volunteered to send a copy of the paper that a doctor in Rochester, New York had written, outlining the use of a couple of medications and zinc. I received the paper just a couple of days later by special mail. I was overcome with hope and joy...God had put together an intricate plan to get this information into my hands. Now I had this information I went immediately to the University Hospital to put it in the hands of the specialist in charge of our case.

When I was called in for the appointment, I was optimistic and anxious for the doctor to see the papers I brought from the doctor in New York. He glanced over the information briefly and asked me why I thought I could come into his office and suggest our daughter was not receiving the best possible care. The appointment was over.

I drove home in a state of confusion; dumbfounded by the reaction of the specialist I thought we could trust to treat Lea. How could this be? The papers outlined a treatment that was making a positive change in the lives of people afflicted with Wilson's Disease in the United States. I prayed!

Two days later, there was a knock on the door of our apartment. When I opened it, a courier was handing me a letter - a letter from the specialist at the University Hospital. I signed for the letter and opened it with apprehension. What else could he say in his opposition to my request for his help?

What I read made my heart soar and I began to praise God for His indescribable goodness! The doctor apologized for dismissing me from the appointment. He recognized that I came to him seeking the best care for our daughter, not to tell him how to do his job. He commended me for taking a stand for Lea and for courage in doing so.

He went on to say that the medication identified in the paper was produced in Britain at a hospital where his sister was a nurse (another *but God* moment!). He said that he had taken the initiative to order the medication and that the University Hospital would cover the cost of it until we could find a method to pay for it.

My husband, a journeyman tradesman, was part of a union and they set up a payment plan with the hospital to cover the nearly $2000 a month for this new medication. Nothing is too big or too complicated for our God!

The next two years of Lea's life were spent rehabilitating from the initial medication and from the brain injury she acquired from the Wilson's Disease. This disease is a congenital degenerative disease of the liver which destroys the liver's ability to metabolize copper, which we take in through our diet. The unmetabolized copper then deposited in the brain, liver, and eyes.

The areas of the brain affected by the copper deposits were involved in Lea's motor skills, emotional stability, and in decision making. When her life was reasonably free from stress, she functioned quite well; but life is not a constant stress-free zone. Lea spent many years trying to regain the time in her life that was stolen from her – years spent in hospital and in rehabilitation facilities. She used humor to "cope", but she had lost much of her ability to make good decision. She lived for the moment and closed a blind eye to the consequences of her actions or was unable to link decisions with consequences.

Lea came home, and we continued the therapy at home. She resisted this and fought it with all her physical and emotional strength. The change in Lea's personality and speech was incredibly stressful for Lynne and it created even more tension in our home. My husband was fighting for some bit of control over the life he could not make sense of...he used alcohol and fury as weapons against anyone who tried to get close.

I was at the end of myself, at the end of my sanity... I attempted suicide and ended up in the hospital. The girls went to stay with my parents, and I stayed in the hospital a short time, during which I found an apartment for the girls and me. Each day, I would move things into the new place and work on making it a pleasant home for us, then return to the hospital for therapy and groups. Finally, I could leave the hospital permanently and bring the girls home from my parents. This was a time of discovering who we were without the turmoil and fear we had lived in for years...it was a peaceful time. We could play the music of our faith and read the scriptures whenever we wanted. It was a healing time for the three of us; however, it was a time to discover new forms of addiction and godlessness for my husband. He spiraled down into dereliction; greater fury; and isolation brought on by his debauched behaviors.

At last, it appeared that he was at the end of himself, and he went into an alcohol rehabilitation program. The girls and I were ecstatic along with our pastors – our prayers were being answered.

He completed the three months rehabilitation, and I was encouraged to reunite with him and move together again. Now, I understand there needed to be a period to work on our relationship and time to ensure the break from alcohol was successful.

We lived for a few weeks in a home free from the madness that addictions bring; then came a slow return to the old ways. During this time, our youngest daughter started complaining of headaches and nausea. After a week or so and no improvement, I took her to the family doctor. He said to let her rest for a couple of days since it was just the flu. She should be back to normal in a short time. She spent a couple of days at home, but she was not feeling better; in fact, the symptoms were worsening. I noticed signs of internal bleeding, and feeling justified after two doctor's appointments, I took Lynne to the emergency unit.

The doctor assessing Lynne ordered an x-ray...when the film came back, the doctor wondered if there had been trauma to her stomach. When I assured him that there had not been, he said that there was, in that case, a large mass in her abdomen. They kept us in the emergency unit until all the specialists could assess her. While we were waiting, I told Lynne that we should plan Christmas since this was November 11 and not long until the holidays. She told me in a matter of fact way that she would not be here at Christmas. I really did not understand what that meant until later.

The oncologist came to see us at the end of a long wait. There had been a meeting of the doctors who assessed Lynne throughout the day...they concurred that she had cancer, and she would need to be admitted to the local hospital until she could be admitted to the University Hospital.

Over a week later, Lynne was admitted to the University Hospital on a Sunday. Treatment was to begin on Tuesday. Chemo would be started to attack the "large cell, non-Hodgkin's lymphoma" which was extremely aggressive. She was swelling as the cancer spread throughout her body. Her faith was intact, and she was still a sweet and jovial young lady who shared Jesus with everyone. Even in constant pain, she was loving and humorous.

On Tuesday morning, my husband and I drove the two hours in silence, not knowing what to expect when we arrived at the hospital. When we walked into the room, Lynne was sitting up with tubes and hoses hooked up to her. When she saw us, she said," there they are". Then she said she wanted to lay down. She was put to bed and they checked her vitals and asked us to leave...before we left, I read a scripture to Lynne (Revelation 21:4, NLT: "...and God will wipe away every tear from their eyes; there shall be no more death, nor sorrow, nor crying. There shall be no more pain, for the former things have passed away.") and prayed with her. We left to allow the team to do what they needed to do. We spent a little while looking at Christmas displays and then we heard a page for us to return to Lynne's unit.

The doctor was waiting for us and took us into a "family room" where others on the team were waiting for us. Lynne was gone! One minute she was to begin her treatment and the next minute she had moved to her Heavenly home. It was beyond my ability to comprehend...I now had a hole in my gut, a big, empty hole. How do you go on? My body knew how to go on living...breathe, breathe, breathe – my spirit will never die, but my mind, will and emotions did not know how to go on. This little person, who had taken so much of my time and energy in dealing with the condition brought on by my use of alcohol was now gone. Oh, I knew where she was. She was with my Heavenly Father and the Lord Jesus that she loved so well...the One she sang about and talked to everyone about. Knowing that was a wonderful comfort; however, there was still the grief that needed to be experienced and worked through...learning to do life with a huge part of it missing. How would Lea deal with this? What about Lynne's Grandma who was so close to her? What would happen to her Dad – how could he go on?

In scripture, we are told that we do not grieve as others with no hope...this hope is knowing that our loved one is not dead in the way that the world thinks of dead. Physical death for a Christian is just laying down our body, then our real self – our spirit and soul (mind, will, and emotions) moves to Heaven. We have the assurance that we will be reunited with them when we too leave our body and move to Heaven. It is a comfort; however, there is a process to move through and bring to completion when we mourn the death of a loved one.

When my body and soul were worn out, my spirit (the part that is in communication with God) took over, and I began to reach out to Him like never before. As I tried to make sense of my life, I began to think of the life of Jesus, and how He had been born to die...He had a Father who loved Him completely...the sacrifice that Jesus made cost Him His life, but our Father God paid an unfathomable price also. I knew this because of the deep pain in my own heart in losing my daughter – how much more God, who is Love, would experience the pain of watching His Son, Jesus die a horrible death – for you – for me – for anyone who would receive Him. I came to understand the depth of love God has for man...each individual man, woman, and child.

The passing of a child is incomprehensible to a parent...it is outside the parameters of what you expect or can accept. Parents are not supposed to mourn their children... it is supposed to be the children who mourn their parents. That is the "right" way for life to unfold. This event left us feeling completely off balance...off balance and empty. We had to learn to live again without Lynne.

My husband moved to Ontario for work, and Lea spent increasingly more time away from home with friends and cousins. She did not appear to be facing the reality that her sister died. I knew that the Lord was showing me this about Lea, and He wanted me to help her accept what had happened to our family. The next few months were difficult for both of us...but finally I saw Lea's acceptance and I felt it was time to explore education that would prepare her for future employment. She met these suggestions with the same furious resistance with which she met rehabilitation to improve range of motion and balance.

My husband's work was finished in Ontario and he moved home with renewed vigor in pursuing the bar scene and extramarital relationships. The abuse continued although not as frequent, and I felt it was time to leave this situation behind.

I went to see a lawyer and I told my husband he needed to be out of the house at the end of the month. He left the house prior to that date, returning only to collect his belongings. Not long after this, Lea decided that she wanted to move in with her Dad. I believe it looked exciting to her. She began to make poor decisions and received no direction from her Dad. Lea soon left her Dad's home and started her life of independence...a sequence of poor and dangerous choices.

His lifestyle took his health and his cognitive abilities quite soon after this, according to his sister and brother-in-law. About three years later, he fell down a flight of concrete steps and sustained a fatal head trauma. Those who were in contact with him said the week prior to his death they had seen a marked change in his attitude toward them, even expressing love to them. This was totally out of character for him, and I believe it was an indication that he had come into a relationship with the Lord. After all, there had been a constant barrage of prayer on his behalf. I believe I will see my ex-husband when I get to my Heavenly home. The devil had a heyday with my husband's life, but he cannot win against our God!

I want, at this time, to say that I do not believe that divorce is God's best plan and I believe that His heart is broken when it happens. I hate divorce and how it scars the hearts of everyone involved. I do believe, however, that God wants women and children to be safe from abuse; He wants his people to live in peace and safety. I advocate for safety, not divorce – sometimes that can only be achieved by the legal action of divorce.

John 16:33 (NLT)
"I have told you all this so that you may have peace in me. Here on earth you will have many trials and sorrows. But take heart because I have overcome the world."

People often ask, "Why do we have trouble in our lives and why is the world in such turmoil?" In the book of Genesis, God gave authority or dominion to man. It was His plan that man should "rule" on earth and spread Eden over the entire planet. Man gave their authority to the enemy when they believed the lies the serpent told them and followed his directions. That transferred the authority or dominion God gave to man over to the enemy...and the world has been paying the price ever since, unless...that is unless you invite Jesus to be the Lord of your life and return your allegiance to God. So, the answer, as I understand the Word of God, is that fallen humanity and people serving "self", have put the world into utter chaos. Often, we suffer because of the choices of others. These are situations we have no control over; however, we can choose to turn it over to God and stay faithful to Him and His will. If we choose NOT to become bitter or unforgiving, then our character is developed...it is our choice. God never brings calamity into our lives, but if we choose to learn from each trial, forgive and walk in love; then He can trust us with more authority in our lives...it's not how many trials we have in life, but how we respond to them. Each person has trials – how will you respond?

Matthew 11:28 (NLT)
"Jesus said, "Come to me, all of you who are weary and carry heavy burdens, and I will give you rest."."

There is only one way to have victory over the trials that are part of this life, and that is to do what the above scripture says to do. Won't you come to Him now, with all your burdens and heartaches. Give Him a chance. He will not turn you away.

CHAPTER SEVEN

THE GOD OF SECOND CHANCES

Soon after my divorce, I married a man who had a past like my first husband's, but he had a wonderful encounter with Jesus and had given his life to the Lord and was baptized in the Holy Spirit. He was sensitive to the Spirit of God, wise, gentle, and loving and I was smitten. We were married soon after that and embarked on a life of joy in the Lord.

Our first line of defence was always the Word of God and prayer. We were blessed with the opportunity to demonstrate the love of God to friends and family who did not have a relationship with the Lord. Ran was ecstatic when our witnessing resulted in his Dad and Stepmom giving their hearts to the Lord and becoming involved in the local church.

We, too, were involved in a local church in the city where we lived and developed good friendships with the pastor and his wife as well as many within the church. We received good Word-based teaching and the Holy Spirit was part of the worship and ministry...we were blessed! I loved our life and I loved my husband so much...too much! You see, I had put Ran in the place of God in my life. Oh, I prayed and studied the Word and participated in many aspects of ministry; however, very subtly there was a shift in my trust for the Lord. I did not realize this until many years later. Thank God that He is forgiving and merciful.

Our pastor, after a few years of working with us and mentoring us, believed he was to send us out to establish a work in another town. We prayed about it, and both Ran and I felt that was God's plan. Not long after that, we moved and along with our employment, we set about the Lord's work. We began having house meetings which were small, but we had good fellowship. These continued for a time but soon no one came. We continued for many weeks with just the two of us. Then our pastor/superintendent felt we should put the work on hold and get involved in a local church to ensure we had fellowship and a pastor over us who would minister the Word.

We did this and were immensely blessed by the teaching and the fellowship of very loving and accepting people in the congregation. We stayed connected in that church while we remained in that town.

We lived there for about four years and continued to deal with issues in prayer and in the Word until one day completely unexpectedly, Ran declared that he would no longer be going to church with me...he was finished with it. I asked him to explain this out-of-character decision, but he refused to discuss it. I believe it to be the first indiscretion, but he did not reveal that to me.

Soon after this, he became mentally ill, which condition continued and worsened over the next thirteen years. He never talked about what happened to make such a radical difference in him and his faith.

We moved back to our "hometown" and he sought the aid of the psychiatric profession, on the referral of a doctor in the previous town. Over the course of the next couple of years, Ran was diagnosed with a complex mental illness, which they felt was a permanent and deteriorating condition. He was labelled "disabled" and that is exactly what he believed, and that is exactly what he experienced. The scriptures talk about this very thing – Proverbs 23:7a (NKJV) "For as he thinks in his heart, so is he." You see, what we choose to believe will become our experience. God has given us a powerful tool – our mind. That is where we make choices as we are guided by the Holy Spirit speaking into our spirit.

I will not go into all the details of the next thirteen years – suffice it to say that my heart was broken each time Ran made new "attachments" to vulnerable females he met in his extended stays in "Psych Units" or Psychiatric Hospital. He pulled further away from me as the years passed and with the distance there was an anger that was developing in him. It appeared that he hated me and my faith...perhaps it reminded him of the relationship he once had with the Lord.

Ran attempted suicide several times, he required much care and frequent hospitalization or assessment by the crisis worker on call. He was heavily medicated and because of numerous electroshock treatments, his memory and cognitive ability was impaired. I was his caretaker while working full time, and the strain was taking its toll. I should mention here that since moving back to our "hometown", I felt I did not have time to attend church with work and caring for Ran. This was a very foolish mistake on my part – my thinking should have been "I cannot afford not to go to church".

At the same time, my Mom left my Dad and charged me with looking after him. Mom was eighty-one years old and Dad, seventy-seven. I felt I did not have time to attend church now, since I was attending to Dad's daily needs. He was opposed to going into a lodge, so I felt that I was the only solution.

During this period of unrest in our lives, Lea's life was unfolding in a series of relationships and crises resulting from her inability to realize the magnitude of possible effects. That would have been tragic in itself; however, she had given birth to two beautiful children. Each child represented a relationship that did not last, and that involved addictions, violence, and trauma. Each time a new relationship developed and ended, usually violently, the children's lives were thrown into upheaval.

Once again, I experienced the return of "old feelings" of pain... pain and regret because I understood that Lea was choosing relationships that she felt familiar with. I had stayed in the first marriage too long, which allowed my girls to witness abuse, threats, and domination – all which Lea now viewed as "normal".

I cried out to God, seeking forgiveness and absolution from my past choices which I saw now playing out in the lives of my daughter and grandchildren. In my pain, I forgot the truth I knew about my Heavenly Father...He forgives when we ask sincerely. What I was inadvertently struggling with was my inability to forgive myself... I did not realize I needed to forgive myself. I was again living in constant pain...after all, I was a failure in two marriages, and I was a failure in parenting and demonstrating God's love and stability to my family.

Lea was being monitored by Child Welfare and the children went for respite on weekends to a Christian family. During one of these visits, the kids related some of the violence they had seen, and they were removed from Lea and her then partner. They were fostered by this couple until an adoptive family could be found. Again, I witnessed a *but God* moment...the family who adopted the children, was Christian.

The family who adopted the children, were, as I mentioned, a Christian family and wanted only the absolute best for my grandchildren. They chose not to have any contact with the family of origin, due to the violence which had taken place in Lea's home. My heart was broken and the hole I experienced in my heart when Lynne went Home, returned. There was huge guilt that I felt for not adopting the children...I simply could not do more for anyone else than I was currently doing. I sought forgiveness again and again. I needed relief for my soul...I needed to forgive myself.

I understood the wishes of the adopting family and gave them my word never to contact the kids or be a problem to them. Finally, over the next several years, my heart has healed, and my contact with them now consists of regular prayer for them and the family that adopted them. I will be united with them in our Heavenly Home. I know this because they were raised in a Christian home, and I have a promise in scripture. Proverbs 22:6 (KJV) "Train up a child in the way he should go, and when he is old, he will not depart from it."

I titled this chapter "A Second Chance", and the second chance was two-fold in nature although I did not recognize it at the time. This was to be a second chance to have a Christ-centered marriage – a base for reaching out to others with the message of salvation and God's love for them. It was also a second chance to step into ministry – the ministry I knew I was called to from a child, and when we were married, Ran was supportive of that calling at first.

After the onset of mental health issues for several years, Ran and I became more like strangers living under one roof. He withdrew into his world online and his chat relationships were much more important and meaningful to him than our marriage. He became a participant in pornography and related online activities. I withdrew into my life of Christian teaching I received online...I do not mean to suggest that I was less at fault for our marriage falling apart. I was equally to blame since I had access to the answer...Jesus. Ran had closed himself off from the Lord.

Just as our marriage was deteriorating, Lea's life and health had taken a major down-turn. The liver transplant she had when she was twenty was needing to be repeated. Her lifestyle choices had taken their toll on her liver and her body in general. The relationships revolving around substance abuse and abuse of her as a person had taken their toll on her mental health. Our contact was sporadic... she would phone when her life was comparatively calm; but when upheaval came, she would change her phone number and not call for months on end.

One day her boyfriend called and said that Lea was in hospital and her condition was not good. I said I would be there in a few hours...back to same hospital where her treatment had begun many years before.

The next few months were spent traveling to the hospital two or three times a week. Ran often made those trips with me...it was such a blessing to feel connected again. Lea was experiencing periods of lucidity during which we expressed to each other our love, seeking the other's forgiveness, remembering good times from the past, and I would pray with her and remind her of God's unconditional love - we prayed to recommit her life to the Lord. These were precious times for us as we simply spent our time basking in the love we held for each other. The years we regretted melted away and we found a place in our hearts I felt was gone forever.

Lea's condition became critical, and the doctors said that if she did not get a liver soon she would not live. Ran and I went to lunch on that day, and I prayed out loud that when we returned to the ward, they would have found a liver for her. The Lord answered immediately – the doctors were just taking Lea to the operating room when we returned from lunch...a liver had been found! Praise God! Ran did not comment on the immediate answer to that simple prayer; but it had to have had an impact on him. I just continued to praise the Lord for His goodness.

Time is long waiting to see your loved one after a surgery like that. Finally, we were paged to the family room outside ICU. The surgery had not been successful...the portal vein ruptured when the surgical team was attaching the liver, and there was nothing to attach the new liver to... Lea was being kept alive by machine and medication as she bled out...we needed to see her immediately!

The next few minutes were painful and precious...affirming our love for her...reminding her that she was going into the arms of Jesus...her sister would be waiting for her... we will be ok, and we will see her soon when we get there. All this as Lea was drifting away from us and toward her Heavenly home. It was a peaceful departure for Lea...it was a wrenching return to a familiar place for me. This was the place where my body knew how to keep living, but my mind could not imagine life without seeing my girls – oh, I knew I would see them both again, but that black hole in my heart was real. I remembered experiencing this before, but the familiarity was not comforting.

I had questions after this unexpected conclusion to Lea's life here. I had prayed, and God had answered so quickly and wonderfully...a liver was available when we returned to the hospital unit after lunch. Why had the operation been unsuccessful...why did God provide a liver when her vein ruptured, making the liver impossible to attach...I had questions...I was angry, and I wondered at the confusing result.

Over the course of the next couple of weeks and three separate memorials for Lea, I had the opportunity to talk with many of her friends and pray for them. I love how open to God people are during times like this and it opens the door for God's love to come in. I was, in turn, grateful for the expressions of love and prayers of my church family. *But God* moments were poured into my life through them.

Soon it was time to go through Lea's things and organize them. I had her journals and un-mailed letters she accumulated. It was during this time that I found some answers to the questions I had around her dying...why God answered some prayers but appeared not to answer others.

As I read through her journals, it became obvious that Lea was not happy in her life, indeed, several times indicated that she wanted to die...be done with this life...go to be with the Lord. This life, and all the many ways that she chose to "numb" her senses to the pain of her decisions, were useless and left her feeling empty and angry.

God answered my prayers as far as He could without violating Lea's choice to leave this life...only a God of love would treat each of us and our requests to Him with such consideration. I am satisfied knowing that God heard and answered my prayers to affirm my faith; and with the same consideration, answered Lea's heart desire to be with Him there in her Heavenly home. What a God! What Love!

Ran did not talk much about Lea's passing, only to question my faith concerning her place in Heaven. He felt that her decisions in life disqualified her - I am so thankful that our place in Heaven is not secured by what we have or have not done; but by what Jesus did in his life, death, burial, resurrection and return to Heaven in victory over sin, death and hell. We only need to receive His gift of forgiveness and give Him permission to dwell in our heart and live through us.

Ran isolated himself from me again, and when we did talk, demonstrated an anger towards me that was at times frightening. One night as I was praying, the Holy Spirit spoke to me that I needed to apply the Blood of Jesus for protection. I dismissed it and continued to pray about other things. A second time the Holy Spirit gave me the same warning. This time I obeyed. After my prayer time, I went to sleep, but was wakened to find Ran standing at the end of the bed watching me. I was praying in the Spirit as I woke up and Ran left the room. God was indeed involved in every detail of my life. Why had He warned me about my safety?

The answer to that would come a few days later, when Ran asked me to take him to the doctor. He arranged, through the doctor, an admission to the mental health facility where he had spent much time previously. The next day, he called me at work and at the request of the psychiatrist, asked me to come to the hospital after work. When I got there, he explained that the psychiatrist insisted that I be told of his plans to "do away" with me. He also at this time, revealed that he had been "involved" with someone.

I did not see a future for us, given the circumstances and told Ran that I would proceed with a divorce.

The months that followed were painful...I was still dealing with Lea's going Home from four months earlier; and now this. As I reflected on our twenty-two-year marriage; I realized that I had lost my assurance of God's love for me and my faith had begun to diminish. You will remember that at the beginning of this chapter I said that I had put Ran in God's place. Of course, I did not do that intentionally; but the result was that I looked to Ran for what I would have sought from God prior to our marriage.

People will always fail us at some point and when that happened in our marriage, I felt that it was God who had failed me. The enemy is so cunning and watchful, and he is willing to wait until just the right time to put doubts in our heart about God's faithfulness. Over time, because I had given Ran the place on the throne of my heart, when he betrayed my trust, the enemy deceived me into believing it was God who had let me down. It was not Ran's fault that my faith was faltering; and I did not realize until years after our marriage was over, what had happened. It happened slowly and insidiously, but the effects of this stealthy plan of the enemy was almost immobilizing at times...*but God!!*

It has been a long journey returning to the place of trusting God's faithfulness and choosing just to believe His Word regardless how the situation looks. I am still on that journey; but I am pleased to say that I am making progress by His Grace. It was never God who let me down – it was my misplaced trust in another human being. God does not share His throne with anyone or anything else, and we are the one who enthrones either God or another.

God will *not* fight for the right to sit on the throne in your heart...*you must choose.*

Joshua 24:15 (KJV)
"...choose you this day whom ye will serve"

Jesus died for the sins of the whole world, but unfortunately, not all the world will be saved. That is because each person must either accept the gift that Jesus has for us or reject it.

You may be thinking that your past is so disgusting that this Man Jesus could never accept you...or you may be thinking that you have been a good person and certainly don't need forgiveness for anything. Well, the Bible says something different.

Romans 3:20-24 (NLT)
"For no one can ever be made right with God by doing what the law commands. The law simply shows us how sinful we are. But now God has shown us a way to be made right with him without keeping the requirements of the law, as was promised in the writings of Moses and the prophets long ago. We are made right with God by placing our faith in Jesus Christ. And this is true for everyone who believes, no matter who we are. 23 For everyone has sinned; we all fall short of God's glorious standard. Yet God, in his grace, freely makes us right in his sight. He did this through Christ Jesus when he freed us from the penalty for our sins."

I want to pray for you if you will allow me:

Father God, I want to bring to You each person who is reading this book. I ask You to speak into their heart and show them Your wonderful love for them. Reveal Yourself to each person and stir each heart to respond to You and receive the gift of Jesus' sacrifice for them.

Jesus is standing outside the door of your heart waiting to be invited in. If that is your desire, please pray the prayer below:

Heavenly Father, I have made so many mistakes and hurt so many people. I am sorry. Please forgive me. Take my life and turn it around and make something of it. I give You permission to make the changes and give me a new heart. Please come in Jesus and be the Lord of my life. I welcome You into my heart and from this day, I will live for You. Reveal more of Yourself to me each day and make Your Word come alive in me. Thank You for paying for my sins, Jesus! Lead me in the paths You have for me. Thank You for saving me...I am born-again!

Other *But God* Moments

I want to take a little time at the beginning of this chapter to talk about the involvement of angels in the life of a believer. I believe that they (angels) are far more involved with us than we may expect.

What does the Bible have to say about angels and their purpose and assignment concerning man?

Hebrews 1:7 (NLT)
"Regarding the angels, he says, "He sends his angels like the winds, his servants like flames of fire."

Hebrews 1:14 (NLT)
"Therefore, angels are only servants—spirits sent to care for people who will inherit salvation."

Daniel 9:20-22 (NLT)
"I went on praying and confessing my sin and the sin of my people, pleading with the Lord my God for Jerusalem, his holy mountain. As I was praying, Gabriel, whom I had seen in the earlier vision, came swiftly to me at the time of the evening sacrifice. He explained to me, "Daniel, I have come here to give you insight and understanding."

Luke 1:28-33 (NLT)

"Gabriel appeared to her and said, "Greetings, favored woman! The Lord is with you!" Confused and disturbed, Mary tried to think what the angel could mean. "Don't be afraid, Mary," the angel told her, "for you have found favor with God! You will conceive and give birth to a son, and you will name him Jesus. He will be very great and will be called the Son of the Most High. The Lord God will give him the throne of his ancestor David. And he will reign over Israel forever; his Kingdom will never end!"

Acts 12:4-17 (NKJV)(excerpts)

"So when he had arrested him (Peter), he put him in prison, and delivered him to four squads of soldiers to keep him. Peter was therefore kept in prison, but constant prayer was offered to God for him by the church. Peter was sleeping, bound with two chains between two soldiers; and the guards before the door were keeping the prison. Now behold, an angel of the Lord stood by him, saying, "Arise quickly!" And his chains fell off his hands. Then the angel said to him, "Gird yourself and tie on your sandals"; and follow me." So he went out and followed him...but thought he was seeing a vision... the angel departed from him...And when Peter had come to himself, he said, "Now I know for certain that the Lord has sent His angel, and has delivered me from the hand of Herod...he came to the house of Mary...Peter knocked at the door of the gate... Rhoda recognized Peter's voice...ran in and announced that Peter stood before the gate...But they said to her, "You are beside

*yourself!... "It is his angel" ... he declared to them how
the Lord had brought him out of the prison..."*

Psalm 103:20-21 (NKJV)
*"Bless the LORD, you His angels, Mighty in strength,
who perform His word, Obeying the voice of His word!
Bless the LORD, all you His hosts, you who serve Him,
doing His will."*

Psalm 91:11,12 (NKJV)
*"For He shall give His angels charge over you, to keep
you in all your ways. In their hands they shall bear you
up, lest you dash your foot against a stone."*

Angels are created by God to work on behalf of people
who are saved or who are on their way to being saved. They
protect us and set up circumstances to fulfill the scripture
in our lives. They live in the spiritual realm; however, they
can make themselves visible to us, allow us to hear them,
and appear like human beings. The angels of God are for
us and not against us, although they can be quite fearsome
in their power. Sometimes they bring a message from our
Father in Heaven to us and sometimes to give us direction
during a difficult period in our life.

On several occasions throughout my life, I have encountered angels. I have never experienced fear during
these encounters... they have appeared as flames of fire,
allowed me to hear their voice, appeared as a huge and
glowing figure who looked like a very large human being,
appeared as ordinary human beings, and at other times I
merely saw or felt their involvement in my circumstances.

The first time an angel allowed me to see him, was
the experience I briefly described earlier in this book. I was

alone in the house; it was dark, and the only light was the piano light. I was practicing my lesson and the light from the angel shining in the dining room caught my attention. The angel was exceptionally large, and I did not see his head because it went up to the ceiling; however, there was no fear attached to this experience – only peace. Think about it... I was about nine years old and the only one home. Quite unexpectedly, there appeared in the adjoining dining room, a huge and shining being. Looking back on the encounter, I am struck by the supernatural aspect of the incident in that it did not instill fear but peace!

The next encounter with a Heavenly messenger occurred when I was under the influence of strong medication and was in a dangerous place emotionally. As I described earlier, I was merely existing, and an angel allowed himself to be heard as I walked towards home. His message to me was to throw away the prescription and I did not experience any of the withdrawals which were part of coming off this type of medication... remember that I do not believe in coincidence – only God incidences!

Some years later, and during a difficult period I experienced another angelic visitor. This time, however, it took a while to determine what had happened. It had been a season of brutal abuse and everyone turned a blind eye to the situation. I was isolated and felt abandoned. I woke in the middle of the night to see a column of flames in the corner about three feet from me. I immediately knew it was not a natural fire which would burn down the house. I did not feel fear – again the encounter brought a peace. The peace allowed me to fall back into a deep and restful sleep. I recognized the heavenly quality of the appearance of flame in the bedroom, but I did not immediately associate Hebrews

1:7 (NKJV) "And of the angels He says: "Who makes His angels spirits and His ministers a flame of fire."

The only time that angels appeared as ordinary men was at the beginning of winter when Lea and Lynne were with me trying to get to our home during a wet and very heavy snowfall. We needed to go up a hill to get home, and the tires were not suitable for this type of weather. As we attempted to drive up the hill with our wheels going forward, we began to slide back down the hill. I told the girls to pray with me for angels to help us up the hill, and immediately, two very ordinary men in lumberjack shirts were pushing the car up the hill. I had a small car but pushing any car on ice uphill was impossible. At this moment, I was not thinking angels because they looked so ordinary. When we got to the top of the hill, I stuck my head out the window to thank them... they were GONE! They were nowhere in sight... they should have been a few feet from the car, but they were gone – then I knew that our prayer for angelic help had been answered... and the girls knew it also.

As I said, sometimes we see the angels in some form or another, and sometimes we feel the effects of their involvement. The incident I will now describe will demonstrate the unseen effects of angels. I had stopped at a red light and when the light turned green, I advanced through the intersection. When I got to the centre of the intersection, a red and black Mini Cooper drove right in front of me and I T-boned her... she had been texting and had driven right through the red light. All I could do was watch as my vehicle impacted with hers, but the most unusual thing happened. When we collided, it was like sinking into a thick pillow. Her door was pushed in and she had to exit through the passenger's door, and the frame of my car was slightly twisted. It had been quite an impact, yet it felt like driving into a pillow; in fact, when we collided, I said out loud "Boy, that was soft!" My glasses were thrown across the car onto the floor and my leg was just a bit stiff the next day... I did not see them, but my angels were on the job protecting me from harm.

A couple of weeks ago, I saw movement out of the corner of my eye and asked the Lord if that was an angel. He answered "Yes", and I asked Him what the angel was doing there. Immediately, the Lord answered that the angel is the "Guardian of the House". I was thrilled to know that I have an angel whose sole assignment is to guard the house and keep us from all the enemy's attacks. (I need to clarify that when I say the Lord answered, I ask the Lord out loud, and He answers in my spirit. I have only heard an audible voice a time or two in my life.)

Today I am overwhelmed as I review these encounters with angels. From early childhood until now the Lord has dispatched angels at critical times – indeed, every day they are watching over me. Psalm 91:11, 12 (NKJV) "For He shall give His angels charge over you, to keep you in all your ways. In their hands they shall bear you up, lest you dash your foot against a stone."

My reason for including this chapter in the book is to encourage and assure you, that even though you may be feeling abandoned or alone - YOU ARE NOT abandoned or alone. If you are born again, the Spirit of God is living in you and He will never leave you. He has also assigned angels to watch over you and keep you in everything you do as we read in the above passage from Psalm 91.

As you read these experiences regarding the involvement of angels in my life, it may trigger a memory which will point to the activity of angels in YOUR life. As you become aware of God's plan to use angels to help you and protect you, I pray that you will see proof in your life of your angelic helpers and security guards. *Do not worship angels, but worship God who has dispatched them to take care of you!

INHERITANCES

Inheritances are usually viewed in a positive light since they bring financial and property increase into the possession of one named in a will; however, there are spiritual inheritances which may or may not be positive.

Negative spiritual inheritances are often called family traits by people who are not aware of the spiritual realm and the existence of the devil and his hatred for God's children.

Deuteronomy 5:9,10 (NLT) "You must not bow down to them (other gods) or worship them, for I, the LORD your God, am a jealous God who will not tolerate your affection for any other gods. I lay the sins of the parents upon their children; the entire family is affected—even children in the third and fourth generations of those who reject me. But I lavish unfailing love for a thousand generations on those who love me and obey my commands." - my addition in parentheses.

You may have heard some people say "Well, cancer runs in my family", or "My family have horrible tempers", or "I come from a long line of child abusers". Most people do not realize they are dealing with "generational sins or curses" (as in the case of cancer or mental illness) which can be dealt with quickly and completely by prayer and applying the Blood of Jesus to that issue and declaring it "finished" in Jesus' Name.

In my case, I dealt with the generational curses affecting me, when I was baptized in the Holy Spirit, as I read and did the work in each chapter of the book "The Holy Spirit and You" by Dennis and Rita Bennett. You may want to go back and reread that chapter in this book.

Do not allow the term "generational curses" to scare you off... it is just a name and remember that the Bible says that Jesus has the Name above every other name. Philippians 2:9 (NLT) "Therefore God also has highly exalted Him and given Him the name which is above every name..."

My inheritance in the negative spiritual sense, was anger, emotional coldness, and abusive behavior in raising my children, substance abuse, fear, and need for control. These were "family traits" that were passed down to my parents from their parents and then on to me. These are not just bad habits like biting your nails or talking loud etc. These are part of who you are until you do something to remove it from your life and prevent you from passing it down to your children.

Many people and I would venture to say, most people, are devastated by the recurring and hurtful behaviors over which they have no apparent control. They try in their natural ability to change, but eventually the inherent concern rears its ugly head again... it is a spiritual issue that can only be removed spiritually.

You will remember from the earlier chapters, that I despised what I did and tried for years to change. What I did not understand, was that it was not what I did, but who I was. I did what I did because that was who I was, that is until I invited Jesus into my heart – I was born again. When we invite Jesus into our lives, He changes our heart... we become a different person and that is why we can leave the old ways behind with His help, by His blood, and in His Name!

There is only one way to remove these from your life and ensure they will no longer be passed on through you... that is to be born again, and to bring these "curses" to the Lord to be washed away by the Blood of Jesus. Be born again and renounce your participation in these "family issues" ... make Jesus the Lord of your life – repent and be baptized. Mark 16:16 (NLT) "He who believes and is baptized will be saved; but he who does not believe will be condemned."

Psychiatrists and psychologists have all kinds of techniques and methods to modify behavior, and these are not effective in bringing an end to aberrant behaviors when it is a heart issue. Mental health professionals want to make a positive difference in the lives of those they serve, but without spiritual knowledge, they are powerless to effect lasting positive changes.

Jesus is exactly who He said He is in John 14:6 (NLT) "Jesus said to him, "I am the way, the truth, and the life. No one comes to the Father except through Me."

Romans 10:9-11 (NLT)
"...that if you confess with your mouth the Lord Jesus and believe in your heart that God has raised Him from the dead, you will be saved. For with the heart one believes unto righteousness, and with the mouth confession is made unto salvation. For the Scripture says, "Whoever believes on Him will not be put to shame."

1 John 1:9 (NLT)
"If we confess our sins, He is faithful and just to forgive us our sins and to cleanse us from all unrighteousness."

2 Corinthians 5:17 (NLT)
"Therefore, if anyone is in Christ, he is a new creation;
old things have passed away; behold, all things have be-
come new...."

Acts 3:19 (NLT)
"Now repent of your sins and turn to God, so that your
sins may be wiped away."

If you find that you are trapped in destructive patterns or recurring cycles that bring harm to you or others, there is a way out, and His Name is Jesus. He will not refuse to set you free and forgive you... all you need to do is ask Him.

I would like to lead you in a prayer for deliverance... that is just a term that means freedom from some prison or something that holds you captive. If you will believe, the chains will fall from your life and you will come into FREEDOM! The only way to receive anything from God is by faith... it is the only way! It may sound complicated, but faith is amazingly simple. God has not asked us to do something hard or impossible; in fact, it is simply choosing to believe what God says in His Word. If thoughts come that bring doubt or fear that it is not true, refuse those thoughts and return your heart to the Word. In the beginning, it is simply making a choice that you will only believe God and His Word. As you spend time reading and thinking about the scriptures, you will find that faith grows. For now, just choose to believe God.

You pray the prayer *out loud* and bring each destructive and harmful recurring behaviour to the Lord. Don't be afraid to say it out loud... the Lord knows about it already, so you won't surprise Him... but it is important that you name each behavior, sinful practice, fantasy, or hate toward another person. As you pray this prayer and name each bondage, see in your heart the chains breaking in that area and see yourself come free. Then name the next bondage and repeat the process for each one. I use this process when praying for people, not because God could not handle the whole package of bondages at one time... it is so that the person has the opportunity to "see" each bondage lose its power and fall off. God is so much bigger and more powerful than we can even imagine. It is we who need to do things in steps and processes, so that we can fathom what has just happened to us.

Let me lead you now in prayer:

Heavenly Father, I thank you for saving me when I asked Jesus to come into my heart and take up residence there. I thank you, Lord Jesus, for dying for me so that I would not have to endure the penalty that my sin deserved. I believe that You are able to set me free from these sins that keep coming up in my life... sins that I hate and sins that hurt others around me. I have tried to get free in my own strength, but I cannot. I do not want to live this way anymore... I am sick of it and so now I come to You to confess my sins and be free and clean.

I confess the sin of _____, and I turn away from it. I bring these chains to You. Please break them off me. I choose to end this pattern in my life and I believe that from this moment my chains are gone, and I am free from

_____, in the Name of Jesus and by His blood. Thank You for setting me free.

Repeat for each area of bondage, and see with your heart, the chains falling off and you walking free.

When you have prayed through all the areas of bondage in your life, it is important that you change the things that will build upon the freedom that God just gave you. For example, if it is the bondage to alcohol that God set you free from, it is important that you do not continue to go to the bar, play around with the occasional drink, or anything that would draw you back into the old ways. Many have lost their freedom to careless treatment of the gift that God gave them. Whatever the bondage was, it is your choice to continue in freedom or just give in and go back to the old way... the choice is yours!

The Bible gives us the answer to stay free and live in the victory that God has given us. If your bondage was outbursts of rage and anger, find scriptures that talk about the opposite of anger.

Proverbs 15:1 (NLT)
"A gentle answer deflects anger, but harsh words make tempers flare..."

Proverbs 22:24,25 (NLT)
"Don't befriend angry people or associate with hot-tempered people..."

Proverbs 29:11 (NLT)
"Fools vent their anger, but the wise quietly hold it back..."

From these scriptures you can begin to renew your mind and continue free. Declarations are helpful in keeping the positive changes in our lives. You could declare, "I am now free from anger and I answer people patiently", or "I am wise because I choose to control angry words", or "I am patience and kind and I respect others."

Every victory in our lives must be enforced by the Word of God... it is the final authority for every believer. Knowing the Word of God is vital for living this life on the winning side, and it is the ammunition against the enemy, the devil. Just as Jesus won over the devil's temptations in the wilderness by using scripture, we can have the same results using scripture.

Matthew 4:10,11 (NLT)" Then Jesus said to him, ""Get out of here, Satan," Jesus told him. "For the Scriptures say, you must worship the Lord your God and serve only him' Then the devil left Him, and behold, angels came and ministered to Him."

Live your life in victory declaring "IT IS WRITTEN"! This is the way to inherit what our Father God has for us. He has only good in store for each of us. (Jeremiah 29:11-14 (NLT)" For I know the plans I have for you," says the Lord. "They are plans for good and not for disaster, to give you a future and a hope.")